CUMBRIA LIBRARIES

3 8003 04774 8660

wol

KT-491-516

Libraries

RECEIVED

-7. AUG 2017

W/TON LIBRARY

WITHDRAWN

12 OCT 2017

Seaton
2/20

Please return/renew this item by the last date shown.
Library items may also be renewed by phone on
030 33 33 1234 (24hours) or via our website

www.cumbria.gov.uk/libraries

Cumbria Libraries

Interactive Catalogue

Ask for a CLIC password

THIS IS FOR MOUTHWASH, SNAKES AND
LADDERS, ANYONE WEARING A SPECIAL HAT,
AND EVERYONE WHO'S AS DYSLEXIC AS I AM.

OXFORD
UNIVERSITY PRESS

Great Clarendon Street, Oxford OX2 6DP

Oxford University Press is a department of the University of Oxford.
It furthers the University's objective of excellence in research, scholarship, and
education by publishing worldwide. Oxford is a registered trade mark of Oxford
University Press in the UK and in certain other countries

Copyright © Elys Dolan 2017
Illustrations copyright © Elys Dolan 2017

The moral rights of the author/illustrator have been asserted
Database right Oxford University Press (maker)

First published 2017

All rights reserved. No part of this publication may be reproduced,
stored in a retrieval system, or transmitted, in any form or by any means,
without the prior permission in writing of Oxford University Press,
or as expressly permitted by law, or under terms agreed with the appropriate
reprographics rights organization. Enquiries concerning reproduction outside
the scope of the above should be sent to the Rights Department, Oxford
University Press, at the address above

You must not circulate this book in any other binding or cover
and you must impose this same condition on any acquirer

British Library Cataloguing in Publication Data

Data available

ISBN: 978-0-19-274602-3

1 3 5 7 9 10 8 6 4 2

Printed in Great Britain

Paper used in the production of this book is a natural,
recyclable product made from wood grown in sustainable forests.
The manufacturing process conforms to the environmental
regulations of the country of origin.

KNIGHTHOOD for BEGINNERS

FROM THE
MOST BONKERS MIND OF

OXFORD
UNIVERSITY PRESS

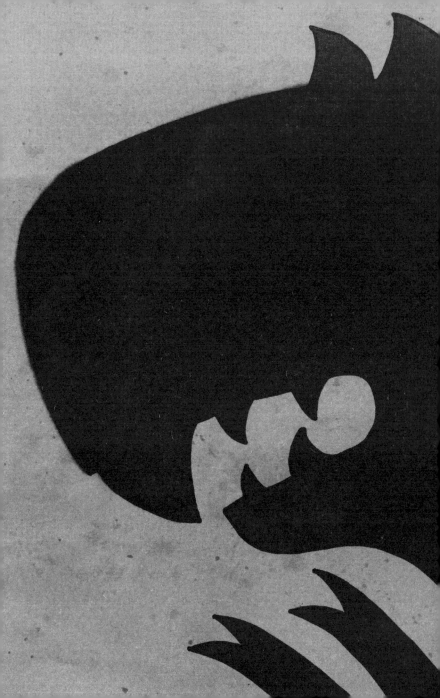

Prologue

There was once a dragon. A dragon called Dave. He lived high in the mountains surrounded by the bones of those who had dared to trespass near the Dragons' Caves. He was the most terrible of dragons, with scales, and teeth, and horns, and feet …

. . . no, wait. Hang on a minute. I don't mean *that* kind of terrible. I mean he was terrible at being a dragon.

You see all dragons must abide by Dragon Lore.

A Dragon must hoard gold, gems, and all riches. He must manage it wisely and keep it tidy.

A Dragon shall riddle and riddle with vigour!

A Dragon must feast on nothing but villages.

A Dragon must knit, because of all the handicrafts, knitting is the fiercest.

To be honest no one really understands the knitting bit but they do it anyway because that's the way it's always been.

Every dragon must master the Lore by the time they come of age and take their Dragon Test. When he's passed the test a young dragon will receive his certificate and become a fully licensed dragon.

No one has ever failed.
But Dave might be the first.

He'd been up all night studying and first thing
that morning Dave's parents came in and said
they needed to have a 'serious talk'.

'Listen Dave,' said his fearsome father. 'As you know you come from a very old dragon family. We're a proud line of the most dragony of dragons. There was your grandfather who had the biggest hoard since records began, Cousin Myrtle who once ate six villages in a row, and your Uncle Kevin who knitted that lovely hat.'

'What we're trying to say,' said Dave's massive green mother, 'is that you've had the finest education, the best knitting tutor a gold hoard can buy, we've taken you to gourmet villages, and taught you our most cryptic riddles. We've tried our best to make sure you're ready, but your father and I both know you've never been the most talented dragon.'

'You spend too much time reading those books and not enough time actually being a dragon!' said Father.

Dave has a bit of a thing about books. It all started when Dave was a baby and his parents went on a village-tasting tour. They left him with his Great Aunt Maud who was a librarian. (Even dragons need librarians.)

It had a big effect on him.

And ever since then Dave feels about books like most people do about their favourite teddy. If they're not a dragon.

Dave's father bent down and looked him in the eye. 'When did you last set fire to anything?! Have you eaten a single village? And you never even finished that bobble hat…'

Mother shot Father a stern look. 'Now, Rupert, we said we were going to be calm about this. David, today is your Dragon Test and it's very important to us that you get your certificate.'

'Get out there and eat a village, son,' said Father.

'And don't forget your yarn!' said Mother.

'Assume your positions!' yelled the Dragon examiner.

Yes I did knit this leotard myself just this morning.

Dave looked at the other dragons. Maybe I don't have much experience, but I've read EVERY book there is, he thought. How bad can it be?'

Pretty terrible as it turned out. Here are some extracts from Dave's report card:

Hoard Management: Dave was very well informed about hoard history but had not collected any gold of his own. Only treasure can be graded. FAIL.

And this was Arnold the Fearsome's Hoard from 1573...

Basic Knitting Skills: Dave's attempts were enthusiastic but ineffective. FAIL.

Riddling 101: Dave was unable to perform his riddle due to stage fright. He was asked to get down before he had a little accident. FAIL.

Village Digestion: Dave did not manage to eat any of the village despite parental encouragement.

He commented that 'it made him feel sicky'. FAIL.

And so Dave became the first dragon ever to fail their Dragon Certificate. He was devastated and so were his parents.

The shame! The SHAME!

At least Uncle Kevin isn't here to see this.

Dave had never felt so ashamed. Or so hungry. (There is no dessert if you don't eat all your village.) Dave knew an uncertified dragon cannot remain in the Dragons' Caves so he would have to leave the mountains forever, for there are no retakes allowed.

Maybe I didn't work hard enough? Was there a book that I missed?

Dave bid his parents a goodbye that was both teary and snotty in equal measure, and made his way down, over the bits of discarded armour and charred bones of people who had foolishly tried to climb the mountain to the

Dragons' Caves. He was just kicking away another helmet covered in tooth marks when he spotted something amongst the rubble.

It was a book.

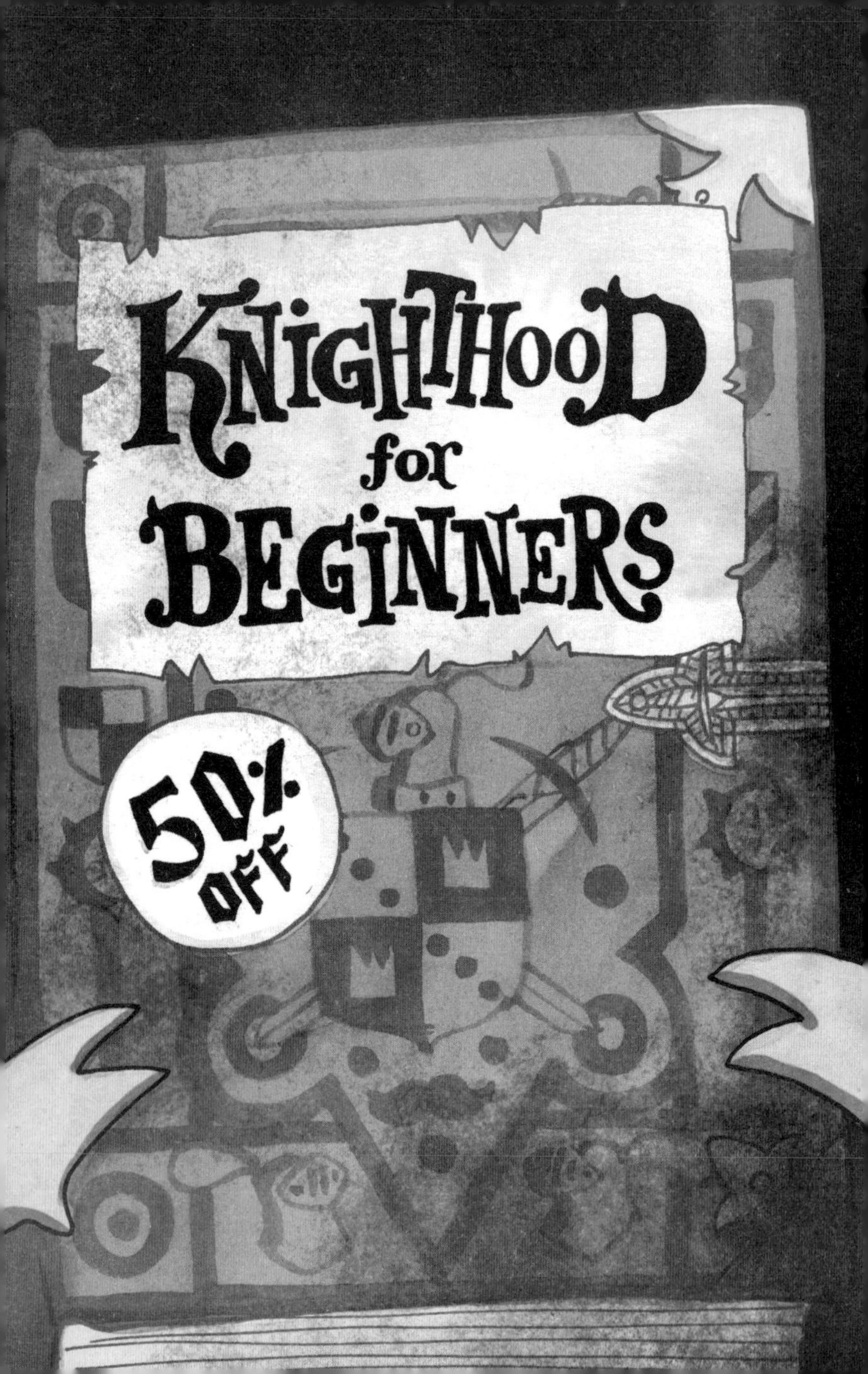
KNIGHTHOOD for BEGINNERS
50% OFF

Dave read the introduction. It was a book about knights. Brave, helpful, kind knights who never had to do any knitting.

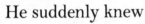

He suddenly knew what he should be doing with his life.

All he had to do was follow this easy-to-use, step-by-step guide.

He plonked himself down and began to read the first chapter…

A Steed Should have:

 fine Physique

 Glossiness

 Attitude

 Good Looks

3 out of 4 will do.

hoosing your trusty Steed

CHAPTER 1

The first thing every knight needs is a Trusty Steed.
Select your steed based on physique, glossiness, attitude,
and good looks. An eye for adventure is a bonus.
Remember, the best knights have the best steeds.

A steed! How do I get one of those? thought Dave. Where do they live when they're not with their knights? They probably hang out in fields swapping stories of adventure, lifting weights, and being fancy! I need to find one and convince it to be MY steed.

Luckily for Dave, the Kingdom did a roaring trade in used steeds so it wasn't long before he came across a field containing exactly what he was looking for.

So many steeds! thought Dave. And I can see the perfect one. He's got all the things the book recommends!

Dave was very excited to have already completed step one.

Dave jumped on his steed of choice.

BAAH!

'Wait! STOP!' yelled the steed, skidding to a halt. 'How dare you! I am Albrecht! Adventurer, Explorer, Trendsetter, and Goat!'

Dave fell off with a bump but he was too shocked even to care because THE STEED HAD SPOKEN!

Ja! I am a very rare talking animal.

remain still whilst I apply the frog...

ribbit?

bah!?

You see I had a run in with a wizard in my younger days...

'But we don't talk about the Wizard thing! It's painful memories. Now how come you can talk mein kleiner grüner friend, and why are you riding me?' said Albrecht.

'Everyone knows dragons can talk!' said Dave. 'We also enjoy riddles, knitting, and occasionally eating villages, but I've not been much good at any of those. I chose you to be my trusty steed because you've got all the things the book said a steed should have. A physique, glossy coat, attitude, and good looks.'

'I am very good looking and glossy,' said Albrecht. 'I was voted Miss Farmyard three years in a row. What is this book that describes me so well?'

Dave showed Albrecht the book. He studied it for some time and Dave was very impressed that not only could his steed talk, but he could read too. And admittedly he was very glossy.

'Knighthood eh? You're training to be a knight, kleiner drache? Why?' said Albrecht.

'Yes! I'm terrible at being a dragon,' said Dave. 'So terrible that I'm the only dragon ever to fail the Dragon Test. If I become a knight I won't

have to hoard gold, eat villages, or knit anything.
I can be brave, helpful, kind, and have adventures!'

'ADVENTURE!' said Albrecht. 'The finest of
things! I do love adventure.'

Once Albrecht had calmed down and stopped
prancing he had a think. 'Hmmmm, I have been
many things but never have I been a steed. You
remind me of my younger self mein Dorf Esser

and I think I can help you on your quest. Enough of the rural life! I will come out of retirement to be your mentor, trainer, life coach, and spirit guide! And trusty steed, of course.'

To be honest Dave was finding this goat a tad confusing, but when you've got a steed this glossy you don't question it.

'I'm sure we'll be a great team,' said Dave. 'Now we should really follow the other steps in the book. Could you help me with number two?'

what's a
spirit
guide?

Acquiring the best Armour

A suit of armour is a must for any knight. The advantage of armour is that it provides protection from all things pointy, and is also conveniently wipe-clean. Make sure any armour can be easily removed in case you should need the toilet at short notice. Armourers can usually be found in towns

WHAM!
fig.1

fig.2
Wipe!

situated near castles. Find your bonus 10% off armoury coupon in the back of this book!

'Aha!' said Albrecht. 'I know where to get armour. We'll need to go to Castletown but we must be very careful small dragon. I have a feeling this might be dangerous for you.'

Chainmail Socks

no more stubbed toes

for low blows

THE

DRAGON'S HEAD

CHAPTER 2

As Albrecht and Dave rode into town it became apparent that this was perhaps not the most welcoming of places.

'OK!' said Dave, carefully tearing the coupon out of the back of the book. 'I'm off to find the armourer. The book says I should tie you up next to a water trough whilst I'm away being knightly…'

29

'Halt impetuous scaly one!' cried Albrecht. 'Are you not looking?! This is not a place of dragon friendliness. Also, Albrecht does not drink from troughs. In my warlord days I used to drink from the skulls of my enemies! Now take cover SCHNELL!'

In a place of safety, Albrecht and Dave discussed their next move.

'I know we dragons have a bad reputation but surely this is overdoing it,' said Dave.

'Perhaps the armourer is a more friendly sort of person? If I explain my quest nicely I'm sure he'll help.'

'No Dave,' said Albrecht. 'I do not think he would help.'

'But this is a disaster!' said Dave. 'The book says I must have armour if I'm going to be a knight. And I don't think I'm a standard size, I'll need armour made to measure! Oh, and the coupon… it's just such a good deal.'

'Do not worry scaly one,' said Albrecht. 'I know how to get you some kleine Dave armour. You stay out of sight and Albrecht will take care of it…'

Town Armourer

DRAGON'S BANE

DRAGON POKER

DRAGON SLICER

DRAGON CRUSHER

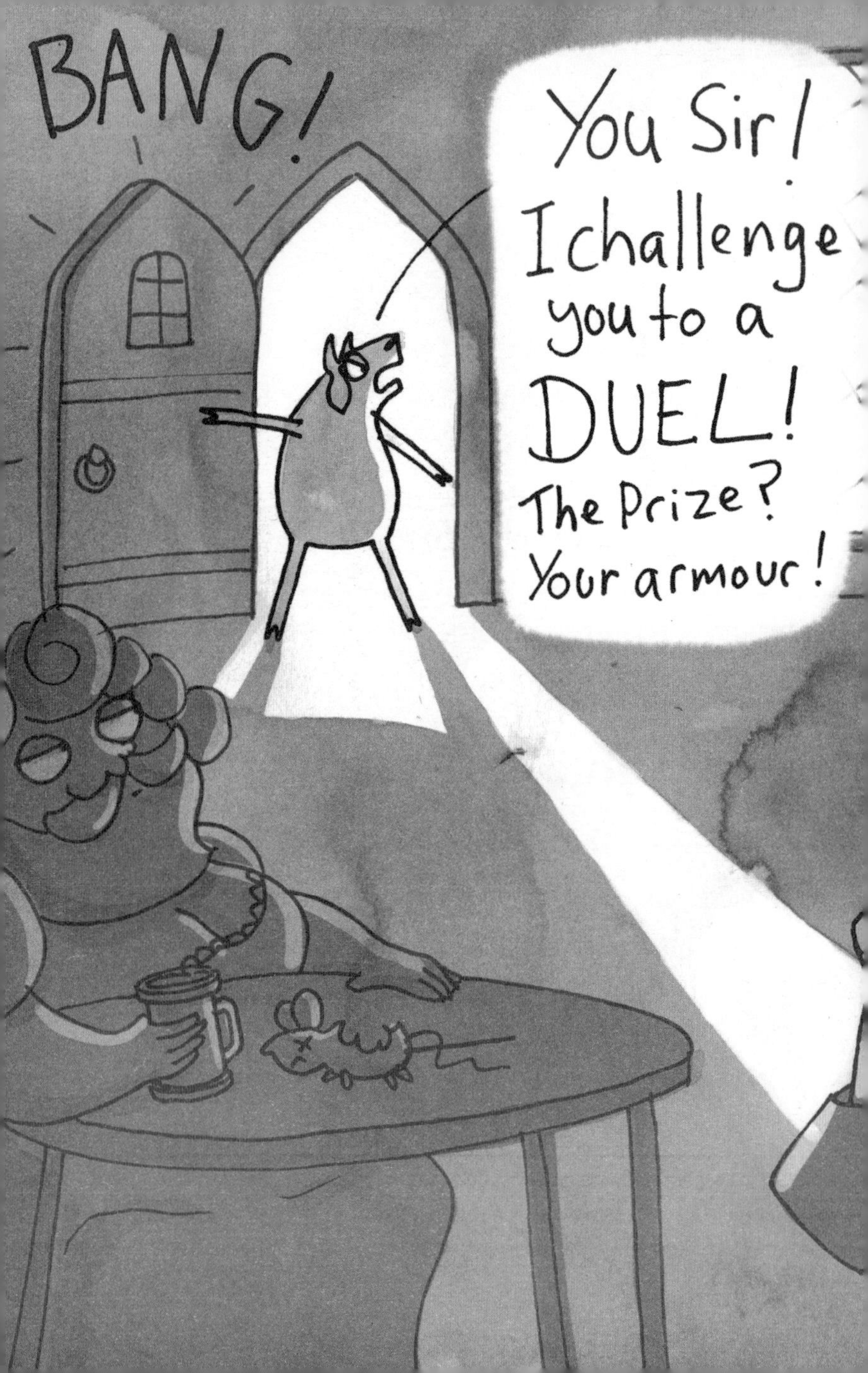
BANG!
You Sir! I challenge you to a DUEL! The Prize? Your armour!

Albrecht knew the mighty battle ahead would require all of his skills. It began with a contest of strength and determination…

…then of style and grace…

…and finally a battle of wits and cunning.

At last Albrecht emerged victorious!

Back outside the tavern Dave was thrilled with his nearly-new suit of armour.

Just as Dave got his moustache on straight he found himself covered by a huge shadow. It belonged to a knight. A big knight. Actually a really massive knight.

'He must have eaten an entire village on his own to get that big!' said Dave.

'Pff he's not that big,' said Albrecht. 'I once knew a whale that was twice the size of him…'

'We didn't steal any armour. My name is Dave, and this is my trusty steed Albrecht, and I'm trying to become a knight…'

'A KNIGHT!' cried Gnasty. 'A tiny, little, green man like you! HA! That's the most ridiculous thing I've ever heard. As the King's Chief Knight and enforcer I'm arresting you both for armour theft, being weirdly green, and smelling kind of goaty.'

'Dave does not smell goaty!' Albrecht yelled as they were marched off.

'Don't worry,' said Dave. 'I've still got the book.'

CHAPTER 3

'Get in there, thieves!' shouted Sir Gnasty as he flung Dave and Albrecht into the disturbingly slimy castle dungeon.

'But really we didn't steal the armour!' said Dave. 'We won it.'

'It was a regulation game of Snakes and Ladders!' added Albrecht.

'Knights just don't steal,' said Dave.

'Stop with this knight talk!' said Gnasty. 'Anyway, I must be off to plot against the King, I mean, er, have lunch.'

And he slammed the door and stomped off down the passage.

'That knight is ÜBER awful but it could be worse,' said Albrecht. 'I was once imprisoned in the tallest of towers. I had to grow my hair so long and convince a prince I was marriage material. Crazy times!'

'That's . . . interesting,' said Dave. 'There must be something in the book about escaping from dungeons.'

Dave pulled the book from its hiding place and started flipping through its pages. 'Yes! Look here. There are even diagrams! I love diagrams.'

Escaping Unfair Imprisonment

During a quest it is not uncommon for even the most experienced knight to become entangled in some misunderstanding resulting in unfair imprisonment. Reasons for imprisonment can include:

- Capture by enemy
- Mistaken identity
- Offending kings
- Parking violations

- Flashy dressing
- Bad dancing
- Picking your nose and eating it

In the case of no conveniently-sleeping jailers or easily-discovered secret passages there's a simple solution. Use your knightly strength! See diagram below:

Fig.1

Fig.2

BAM!

Huzzah!

Dave hauled himself up and fixed his gaze on the door. 'OK. I'm going to do this. I'm going to use my knightly strength!'

'Meine Dave,' said Albrecht, 'that door is very big and solid and you are so small and green ...'

But Dave had already stepped back ... he focused... then he ran like the wind ... and gave a mighty leap ... !

'Ow,' said Dave.

You are lucky you are wearing armour dummkopf.

Prod.

Before Dave could see straight again, the door creaked open and in walked the jailer with their evening meal.

'Good evening prisoners,' said the jailer. 'We have a wide selection of slop available today. There's the Classic Brown slop, always a favourite. The 1542 Chunky Yellow, an excellent vintage. The XXX Super Hot Chilli slop, not for the faint-hearted. If you're feeling brave, we have Mystery Slop, and today's Slop of the Day is: Green.'

'I'll take a bowl of the 1542 Yellow and a XXX Super Hot for my fiery friend,' said Albrecht.

'Very good, sir. Welcome to the dungeons and I hope you enjoy your stay,' said the jailer, locking the door behind him.

'But we don't need slop!' said Dave. 'We need to escape!'

'If life has taught me anything it's never say no to a free bowl of slop,' said Albrecht, enthusiastically eating the chunks out of his Yellow. He handed the other bowl to Dave.

'I'm never going to be a knight if I'm stuck in here!' Dave flung his bowl across the room. It smashed into the ground with an appropriate SLOP! noise and Dave went to sulk in the corner.

Albrecht was only halfway through his slop (he still wasn't 100% sure what the chunks were but they had a not unpleasant fish/socks/breath mint flavour to them) when he heard a sizzling sound coming from the floor.

He turned to look. 'Dave my kleine Suppe Werfer! With your XXX Super Hot Chilli slop display, I think you found our way out. GENIUS!'

CHAPTER 4

In another part of the castle, Sir Gnasty had chosen the King's bathtime as the perfect moment to launch his evil plan.

Huge sack? Check!... Net? Check!... Rope? Check! Excellent. Now we're totally ready to complete my evil plan to kidnap the king and make the kingdom mine! With me, army of evil!

Just as Dave and Albrecht slid their way up a drainpipe and out into the light, Gnasty and his Army of Evil crashed through the King's bathroom door.

Everyone looked a little shocked.

'How did they get in here?!' said Gnasty. 'We can't possibly stage this kidnap in front of witnesses . . . ! Erm, I mean your Majesty! I was just waiting to be of assistance and definitely not plotting your downfall. Let me deal with those prisoners.'

Albrecht shook toilet water off his now not-so-glossy coat and addressed the King with an overly fussy bow. 'Your Majesty, I must throw myself upon your mercy! I am but a simple goat/steed/life coach accompanying young Dave on his quest to become a knight…'

'Sire, they are thieves!' Gnasty butted in.

'I won that armour fair and square!' shouted Albrecht getting angry. 'Sir Ironpants is a rubbish snakes and ladders player!'

How dare you insult my snakes & ladders skills! This means fisticuffs!

He's not worth it Albrecht!

'Wait!' said Dave. 'Your Kingness Sir! If I could just have a word? My dream is to be a knight. I've been reading a lot about them and knights are good, kind, and honest so I wouldn't ever steal! Is there some way I can prove myself?'

'Hmmm,' the King considered. 'I like the way you toilet chaps work. I'm impressed by your daring, if stinky, escape from my dungeons, and I admire your pale green complexion.'

'If you can beat all my knights in single combat then I will make you a knight, Dave my boy. Tomorrow I will hold a Tournament!'

'Is that a thing?' Albrecht asked Dave.

Dave gasped. 'Yep, look here, under "special circumstances". If you win a tournament, the King has the power to grant an instant knighthood.'

 **Tournaments, single combat and hitting with swords.**

for a tournament you will need

A fancy tent
To hang around in before and after fighting.

your Steed
looking their most glossy.

Many Weapons

CHAPTER 5

Early next morning, Dave was already up
and studying hard .'I've been reading about
tournaments and single combat and hitting people
with swords. There's so much to learn. Just look
at all this…'

Turn the page for some

Handy Hints and Tips

Always do your stretches

make sure you're well matched to your opponent.

Swords: Don't hol the pointy end.
ow!

Eat a good breakfast.

Be sure to impress the princesses!

IT is very bad manners to stab your opponent in the back.

And remember, ther is nothing more Knightl than to remain brave, fight to the end and st on your steed no matte what.

Avoid maces at all costs.

Pack spare underwear.

'And that's just one page!' said Dave.

Albrecht snatched the book away. 'Dave, as your trusty steed I am confiscating this book! We do not have to do things the dummkopf knight way. We shall solve this using our GENIUS, not ridiculous hitting.'

Dave was about to protest but it was time to head out to the jousting field.

Waiting for the tournament to begin Dave was feeling incredibly nervous without the book. 'But Albrecht we're not knights, we don't know how to win a tournament! If I could just check a few things about hitting with swords...'

'Worry not, scaly one,' said Albrecht. 'Everyone has a weakness. Let's study our opponents and see what we can learn.'

And of course **Sir Gnasty**

Dame Hilda
Most terrifying beauty of the age

These knights don't seem much like the ones in the book, thought Dave, as he watched Sir Ironpants do another set of disturbing lunges. So they went to have a look at the other knights.

'See meine Dave, dummköpfe!' whispered Albrecht. 'I have a plan for nearly all of them…'

Just then, he was interrupted by the sound of trumpets.

Ladies, gentlemen and peasants! Welcome to the tournament. Today we shall witness Wannabe Knight Dave battle all my Knights in a trial by Combat! Peasants please remember no spitting, keep your boils to yourselves and all Rat-on-a-stick is eaten at your own risk.

First came Sir Ironpants who was very ticklish without his armour.

Then Sir Snoz who had terrible hayfever.

Sir Mightybrow was nothing without his glasses.

Sir Butterball had a big soft spot for his pie.

The mighty lungs of Dame Hilda were almost too much for Dave and Albrecht.

But Albrecht found another use for Butterball's pie.

Thrilled with their victories, Dave could almost smell the knighthood.

'This is going rather well,' said Dave.

REAL KNIGHTS JOUST!

CHAPTER 6

With just one knight left to vanquish Albrecht explained his plan for Sir Gnasty, involving beards, mice, and hairspray, but Gnasty had a surprise for them.

Albrecht looked perturbed. 'I had a plan to defeat one huge Gnasty, but a huge Gnasty, on a massive horse, with a super long, pointy stick? I can see no weakness here!'

Dave went pale and felt a lot like he needed a wee.

But wait… if he was a proper knight he wouldn't just go for a wee. He'd fight Gnasty with his big horse and his big stick anyway. It was time to use some of that bravery the book talked about.

'OK, Albrecht, I remember something about having to "stay on your steed no matter what" so I'll hang onto you with everything I've got and we'll work out some way of knocking Gnasty off his horse.'

When the joust began, Albrecht and Dave weren't doing so well.

71

But Dave refused to let go of Albrecht, even when Gnasty gave them such a whack with his lance that they flew straight up into the air. Gleeful, Gnasty listened to the crowd's applause and waited for his opponents to hit the ground so he could give them an even bigger whack.

But they didn't come down.

Gnasty looked puzzled for a moment then broke into a huge grin. 'I jousted them so hard I smashed them into oblivion! I'm so talented, so amazing, so STRONG! Look at my quads!'

QUADS!

As Gnasty flexed his muscles for the crowd, Dave and Albrecht were having a hasty conversation above him.

'I can't hang on for long!' said Dave.

'Eugh, if you let go we'll hit the ground and that dummkopf will whack us again!' said Albrecht, wriggling.

Dave's eyes widened as he had a brilliant idea. 'But maybe we don't have to hit the ground! Brace yourself, I'm letting go.'

How much do you weigh!?

Your feet are so pointy!

73

'Oh now look at
that. Dave is the
WINNER!' declared the King.
And the peasants went wild.

Dave scrambled down from the heap, but before he could check on Albrecht, Gnasty hauled himself up and bawled at the King. 'THEY WERE OBVIOUSLY CHEATING! That's not how you knock a knight off his steed!'

'And he gave away my pie!' joined in Sir Butterball. 'That's just not right.'

Soon all the knights were accusing Dave of cheating.

'SILENCE!' said the King. 'All right then, we'll settle this once and for all. I hear there's a peasant uprising in town. They're nothing but trouble those peasants. Gnasty, you and Dave will go down there and the first one to stop the rioting will be the winner and I'll make them *Chief Knight*!'

'That sounds wunderbar,' said Albrecht, 'and also I may need medical attention…'

CHAPTER 7

As they rounded a corner to see the Dragon's Head tavern, things didn't look great.

Dave flinched. 'Oh dear me, there's some dirty fighting going on here.'

'Dirty? Ha!' said Albrecht. 'When I was a professional mud wrestler we did the dirty fighting. This is all squeaky clean.'

Gnasty came barrelling down the hill behind them and ran straight into the crowds of flailing peasants. 'You want a riot do you?!' he shouted. 'I'll punch the riot right out of you all!'

BE LESS VIOLENT!

'We have to do something fast before someone really gets hurt,' Dave said, getting concerned. 'I'll just have a very quick read of the book.'

Oh my!

Peasants and their habits

Peasants are smelly

... weird ...

and obsessed with Rat-on-a-stick.

They are constantly brawling with each other and there's only one way to solve it.

talk with your Fists!

Dave read the page perhaps a little too quickly. 'Right, it… um… says something about talking to them. That seems sensible. I'll go over there and have a chat with that man hitting that other man with a chicken.'

Albrecht thought this would probably lead to Dave also getting hit with a chicken, but Dave was already chatting.

'Hello Mr Peasant Sir, what seems to be the problem?' said Dave.

The peasant, known in the town as Boil Man mainly because of his boils, was so shocked at being spoken to nicely by a knight he dropped his chicken.

'Well… err…we're dissatisfied with our healthcare system!' Boil Man told him. 'The doctor is terrible!'

'The only thing we can do is BRAWL!' added Carbuncle Guy, happy that he was no longer being hit by a chicken.

'This does not bode well for meine hintern,' said Albrecht. 'How bad is this doctor?'

Boil Man explained.

We're starting to think he doesn't know what he's talking about.

'Pah, I'd make a better doctor than him!' said a massive woman with an even bigger beard (that's right, beard) startling Boil Man and Carbuncle Guy so much they scurried off back into the brawl.

'Would you?' said Dave.

'Well, yes, actually. Watch this.'

'My hintern hasn't been in such trouble since the cannibalistic Sheep Men of Bahbahland ate my tail! I have a wooden one now . . . but how did you learn medicine hairy lady?'

And so the Bearded Lady began to explain.

Ever since she was a girl the Bearded Lady had been forced to earn her living by sitting on her stall and charging people to ogle, tug, or run

screaming from her beard. Her stall bordered the first aid, counselling, and aromatherapy sections of the bookstall next door. She used to read the stock whilst the people pointed and screamed. Gradually she picked up quite a wide range of medical skills. There was one rogue book on fly-fishing in there, so she's not too shabby at that either.

'I wish I could open a clinic,' she said, 'but who would want to be treated by a bearded lady?'

'You could shave?' suggested Albrecht.

The Bearded Lady looked furious. 'I came to terms with the fact that I'm a bearded lady years ago and I won't change just because people are narrow minded. Plus, this is the most luscious beard in the whole kingdom. It's a work of art!'

'Maybe you could team up with the doctor?' said Dave. 'Let's go and talk to him.'

'Don't forget about the task Dave!' said Albrecht.'Who would not want to help this lovely hairy lady but we can't let Gnasty win.'

'But if we can solve this doctor problem we can stop the riot.' said Dave. 'What have we got to lose?'

Got
UNWANTED
LEECHES?
Contact the
Doctor
Jill Paymoney
Delicious
RAT-
ON-A-
STICK
he Ama

CLOSED

CHAPTER 8

DOCTOR

No boils   No plague   No teeth
NO Timewasters!
REASONABLE RATES

50% OFF leech treatments

Dave peeked round the door and said, 'It doesn't look like there's anyone home.'

'Hmm you are correct Dave. Is he in the back having a tea break maybe?' Albrecht went over to a curtain covering a door at the back of the room and pulled it open. 'MEINE GOTT! What is this?!'

'DON'T LOOK AT ME!' shouted the Doctor. 'I'm so ashamed!'

'It's just that I've always wanted to be a fool. The glamour, the applause, the hat, the bells! I made my own costume and I can nearly do a headstand. Don't tell my patients though! I'd lose my position…'

'Do you like being a doctor?' asked Dave 'You don't seem that into it.'

'Gosh no!' said the Doctor. 'It's terrible. All those peasants with all their giant boils and plague everywhere. I mean literally EVERYWHERE. You should see Boil Man's backside…'

'OK STOP!' said Albrecht. 'Could you become a

full time fool?'

'I can't, I just can't!' said the Doctor. 'I'd lose my leeches! They're the one thing that's made being a doctor bearable.'

The doctor really loves his leeches. They do so much together:

Go for long walks in the country.

Have candle-lit dinners.

And stay up late reading poetry.

'That's a bit weird,' said Dave.

The Doctor explained that if he quit, the leeches would have to go to the next doctor and that would break his heart.

The Bearded Lady scoffed. 'That depends on your methods! I operate a leech–free practice because there are some schools of thought that suggest leeches are icky.'

The Doctor scowled and hugged his jar of leeches closer. Then he gasped. 'Wait, you practise medicine without leeches? So I could keep my leeches?'

'Surely this means we could arrange something so everyone's happy?' said Dave. 'Doctor are you actually any good at fooling?'

The Doctor responded by telling them a terrible joke about shark-infested custard whilst not quite managing a headstand.

'That was terrible,' said Albrecht. 'But it is probably better than his doctoring. Dave, do you have a plan and is this going to stop the riot?'

'Yes! Albrecht I'll need your help. Are you much of a performer?'

'Pfff are you kidding?!' said Albrecht.

Back at the Dragon's Head the peasants were rioting, despite Gnasty trying to brawl them into submission. Just as it was starting to look like Boil Man might burst a boil, there was a loud GOOOONG! sound and everyone turned to look at a makeshift stage constructed from boxes. Albrecht leapt into view.

Ladies, gentlemen. and peasants. May I present the one and only DR HILARITY AND HIS AMAZING PERFORMING LEECHES!

The peasants immediately stopped brawling and fell about laughing. Even Gnasty giggled at the shark-infested custard joke. Sharks? In custard? Absurd!

While the crowd was distracted the Bearded Lady, assisted by Dave, quietly snuck up on any peasant in need of medical attention. Before they had a chance to run off screaming or even give the beard an ogle, she slapped plasters on wounds and creams on boils, and in some cases just forcefully recommended a good bath.

Afterwards Boil Man came up to Dave, Albrecht, and the Bearded Lady. 'Brilliant! That man's a much better fool than a doctor. And did you see that leech on the unicycle?... just amazing! Also that cream the hairy lady gave me has done wonders for my boil. It's shinier than ever now. I'll be going to her with all my problems, there'll be no more rioting round here.'

'AAAAHHH!' A blood-curdling yell cut across the square as Gnasty realised that he'd officially lost the competition and with it the title of Chief Knight.

He stormed over to Dave and Albrecht. 'You interfering little pains in the backside! I'll get you next time and when I do I'll smash you so hard you'll ...'

But before it could get ugly he was interrupted
by Sir Ironpants sprinting down the street.
'The Princess! Something's happened to her!
Something terrible. We need all the knights back
at the castle. Now!'

RUBELLA'S ROOM

KEEP OUT!

CHAPTER 9

Back at the castle a full Code Pink emergency was underway. Princess Rubella had fallen into a

Lip balm?

magical slumber and the King had locked himself in her bedchamber and was refusing to let anyone in.

Outside the bedchamber an orderly queue had formed of knights swigging mouthwash waiting to bestow the magical kiss that would wake the princess.

Dave and Albrecht made their way to the door but Gnasty, who had been practising kissing on the back of his hand, spotted them and blocked their way. 'Queue jumping, eh? I can't have you two getting in the way of me awaking the princess and getting back in the King's good books! I'll deal with you once and for all.'

Now this is tasty.

MINT

Gnasty flung his mouthwash at Albrecht and made a grab for him but he was stopped in his tracks by a small voice coming through the bedchamber door.

'Dave? Is that my best knight Dave? Let him in at once but the rest of you kiss-mad knuckle-heads stay outside!'

Inside the bedchamber, safe from Gnasty, Dave saw that the King was in great distress. 'Oh my beautiful Rubella! This is all my fault! I should never have married that terrible woman!'

'Which woman?' said Dave.

'The Wicked Witch!' said the King narrowing his eyes. 'Ever since the divorce she's been trying to get back at me. She didn't even tell me she was a witch, though I suppose all that flying about on brooms and chatting with magic mirrors should have been a give-away.'

'Ah, affairs of the heart are never simple,' said Albrecht, sipping his newly-acquired bottle of mouthwash.

...but she was more woman than I could handle.

Yes that's all well and good but I'm trying to explain about Rubella!

'Where was I?' said the King. 'Oh yes! The witch always hated Rubella. She was a terrible stepmother, and now she keeps trying to give my Rubella a terrible poison that will cause a hundred years' slumber... USING FRUIT!'

'Not fruit!' said Dave.

'First she tried planting a poisoned apple'

'Then a poisoned orange.'

'A poisoned banana.'

'Poisoned cherries.'

'And even a poisoned watermelon.'

'Then that terrible woman changed tactics and left Rubella a poisoned . . . PORK PIE!'

I found poor Rubella curled up asleep covered in pie grease. Now the traditional way to wake her up is with a kiss from a handsome prince but frankly none of those beardy idiots outside will do. And just after we'd got past the whole compulsive frogkissing thing…'

'Is there any other way to break this curse?' asked Dave.

'Well, I suppose the witch could lift it, but there's no way that hag would do it!'

'I could try to talk to her,' said Dave.

'Do you think you could convince her, Dave old boy?' said the King. 'If you do I'll make you the finest knight that ever lived! With your own castle and . . . and a . . . special hat!'

'A special hat?!' said Dave, 'Oh my!'

Oh this thing? That's just my SPECIAL HAT. You know. For being an awesome knight.

DAVE

CHAPTER
10

KEEP
OUT!

Dave trotted up to the witch's cottage and
knocked on the door. Slowly it creaked open and

the witch loomed out of the doorway.

GUTEN TAG!

Hello. Could we have five minutes of your time please?

Dave ducked to avoid a bat and said, 'Er, hi. We were hoping to have a quick chat with you about the King?'

'That tiny little idiot!' the witch hissed. 'I just knew he'd freak out if I told him I was a witch.'

'I can see you're angry,' said Dave, 'but maybe you'd feel better if you moved on? He's not worth it and you deserve better. Maybe it's time to start dating again?'

The witch explained that she was quite busy these days running a new business designing candy cane conservatories but admitted dating could be fun.

'Wunderbar!' said Albrecht. 'I used to be a professional matchmaker so I shall set up some blind dates.'

Nibbles?

That night, at the Dragon's Head tavern, emotions were running high.

Date one was not a success.

Date two wasn't much better.

But date three was very, very different.

'Nice work, chaps,' said the witch. 'Ironpants and I are off on a mini-break in the country.'

'Wait!' said Dave. 'We really need to know how to wake up the Princess Rubella.'

'Oh fine, I don't even care any more! Just use this.' The witch flung something loud and round at Dave as she rode off into the sunset with Ironpants.

Rubella wasn't actually very happy to be woken up and demanded that she have 'just five more minutes,' but the King was thrilled.

'You are just about the best knight we've ever had young David! So brave, so clever, so green. I can't believe we had that big lummox Sir Gnasty as Chief Knight,' the King chuckled.

Gnasty, who had been listening at the door, went a deep shade of purple and stormed off.

'Dave!' said the King. 'Tonight, I'm going to hold a feast in your honour and there I shall make you Knight of the Special Hat!'

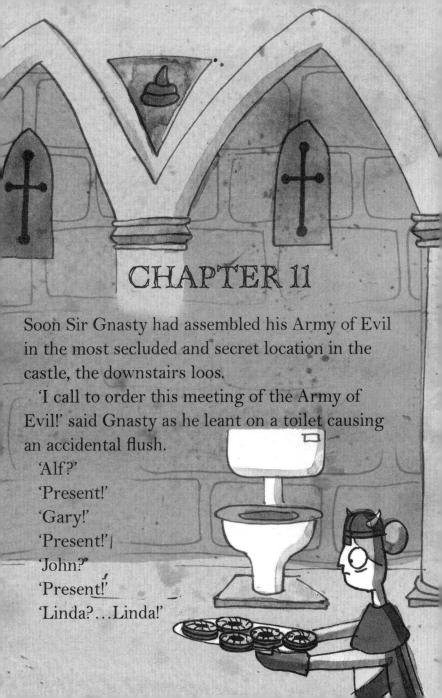

CHAPTER 11

Soon Sir Gnasty had assembled his Army of Evil in the most secluded and secret location in the castle, the downstairs loos.

'I call to order this meeting of the Army of Evil!' said Gnasty as he leant on a toilet causing an accidental flush.

'Alf?'

'Present!'

'Gary!'

'Present!'

'John?'

'Present!'

'Linda?...Linda!'

'She's just getting the biscuits, O Mighty Lord of Evil,' said John.

'It is unacceptable to be late to a meeting of the Army of Evil!' raged Gnasty. 'What kind of biscuits?'

'Jammy Dodgers I think,' said John.

Gnasty considered this. 'Good. So, first item on today's agenda is sharks! Have you acquired the sharks? When the kingdom is mine and I've taken over this castle it's definitely going to need sharks in the moat or it just won't be evil enough.'

John looked worried. 'Not yet Sire but Alf was thinking he'd go down the pet shop tomorrow and ask…'

'UNACCEPTABLE!' roared Gnasty. 'Get me sharks immediately, or I'll feed you to them as soon as we have some!'

'Yes Your Meanness,' said John as he tore off a sheet of toilet roll to mop away the sweat.

'Now, the second item,' continued Gnasty. 'How's my ingenious plan to kidnap the king going? Soon I shall make him sign the kingdom over to me!'

'Hurrah!' roared everyone, nervously.

'And third. That new wannabe knight Dave has to go! Also, I really want his special hat.'

'It is really special Sir,' said Gary.

'SILENCE! It seems this Dave can't put a foot wrong, always following the instructions in that book, "Knighthood for Beginners". I'm sure I have a copy somewhere, I'll have to fish it out. He must have a weakness . . . Go and spy on him my evil army! Bring me any information that could lead to Dave's DOWNFALL! We need him out of the way,' said Gnasty, rubbing his hands together in classic villain style.

'Yes Sir,' said the Army of Evil all together.

'Excellent! That concludes today's meeting,' said Gnasty. 'Now hand me those Jammy Dodgers.'

No not for you.

Sir Dave! you're just so green!

Sign my chest Sir Dave!

CHAPTER 12

At the feast Dave was beside himself with glee. It was a seriously super party with good music, copious mead, and rat-on-a-stick for everyone. And, best of all, everybody was being so nice to him.

Dave was thinking he'd really done it. He'd become a brave, clever, and respected knight. Maybe if he kept following the book he could even become the greatest knight of all time? Perhaps minstrels would write songs about him? Or paint a portrait of him riding Albrecht, looking noble? Or… hang on, where was Albrecht?

Dave spotted him sitting in the corner.

Something wasn't right. Dave went over to see what was wrong and Albrecht hustled him out onto the balcony where they could talk in peace.

'Meine Dave, watching you enjoy this discoteque, strutting about in your special hat has me all of a worry,' started Albrecht, looking out into the night. 'I have a feeling in my tail that you need to stop worrying about what those metal-headed dummköpfe think of you and following their foolish knight rules and believe in Dave. I did say I would be your life coach, ja?'

Dave didn't look convinced. '*I thought your tail was wooden*? And can't you see, Albrecht, the book worked! I used to be a dragon…but now I'm a knight. Dragon…Knight!'

Dave straightened his moustache. 'Why would I do things differently if it works? And I think I'm pretty good at being a knight now. Look! I've got the special hat and everything!'

Albrecht didn't seem impressed. 'I like Dave more when he's being Dave, not a dragon or a knight in a special hat…'

'You're being a big old worry goat. Let's go inside and enjoy the feast.'

But they hadn't been alone out on the balcony.

Sir Dave is a WHAT?!..

Back inside, Albrecht noticed Linda scurry across to Sir Gnasty who had been angrily stomping on some canapés. As she whispered something to him Gnasty stopped stomping, gave a wide grin, and started striding across the room. Before Albrecht could figure out what his game was Gnasty had walked right up to Dave.

'Sir Dave!' he began, and Dave turned to look at him a little nervously. 'You have truly proved yourself to be a brave, wise, and clever knight having fairly beaten me in all your trials. Now we're all gentlemen here.'

Dame Hilda gave an expectant cough.

'… and Ladies of course. We can let bygones be bygones. Why don't I show you where the Chief Knight sits? Up on the top table right next to the King!'

Dave was quite thrilled. If he'd earned the respect of Sir Gnasty he must be a serious knight.

Everyone was clapping as Dave walked up to the top table, but Albrecht pushed his way through the crowd.

'Dave!' said Albrecht breathlessly. 'This is very suspicious! When a mean man called Gnasty starts being nice you have to ask questions...'

'Out the way greasy goat!' shouted someone in the crowd. Albrecht went a bit red and looked at Dave expectantly.

'Albrecht get out the way!' said Dave. 'This is a big moment for me and you're being kind of embarrassing.'

Albrecht, humiliated, stepped back muttering '... it's not grease . . . it is my natural glossiness.'

Dave took his seat at the top table between Gnasty and the King. He felt a little star-struck.

The King struggled up onto his chair and began his speech. 'Ladies, Gentlemen, Knights, and Princess Rubella who shouldn't be here because it's way past her bedtime! I welcome you to this feast in honour of Sir Dave! I'm proud to officially award Dave his knighthood for being especially brave, incredibly wise, astonishingly green-skinned and...'

He's a DRAGON!

127

'That's right! He's a princess-eating, gold-stealing Dragon!' said Gnasty triumphantly.

Everyone in the room gasped and started muttering. The King gave a little shriek as Sir Butterball fainted and Princess Rubella started eating all the pork pies while no one was looking.

Dave looked around the room at all the shocked and angry faces and felt himself starting to panic. 'I've never done any of those things! Yes I'm a Dragon but I'm not even a very good one! What I really want to be is a knight which is why…'

Gnasty started laughing maniacally. 'You can't be a knight! You idiot Dave. Have you even read the final chapter of "Knighthood for Beginners?"'

Dave looked down at the book he was still holding. 'No… some of the pages at the back are a bit burnt…'

'Well I think it's time you did,' said Gnasty. He pulled out his own copy and showed Dave the final chapter.

HOW TO SLAY A DRAGON

CHAPTER 13

Every knight's worst enemy is a dragon. They're dangerous, eat princesses, and their knitting is terrible. It is every good knight's duty to slay them and take their gold.

 They hate Villages

They eat all the gold.

 They set things on fire.

'Oh my, no!' said Dave. 'That dragon looks like Great Aunt Maud!'

People started to scream and panic. Gnasty began chanting 'SLAY THE DRAGON! SLAY THE DRAGON!' and a good few knights were starting to join in. Dave couldn't believe it. Good, kind, brave knights killing dragons? He felt numb.

The only person not in a panic was Albrecht. He knew he'd have to cause a distraction. Fast.

Albrecht leapt into action.

While everyone was watching Albrecht, Dave tore his slightly stunned eyes away from the performance and made a quick escape out of the castle.

After a couple of numbers, Albrecht also decided it was time to make a swift exit, even if his fans had other ideas.

Emerging outside the castle walls, Dave was already working out a plan.

'I know this looks bad Albrecht, but if we can somehow make it look like I've slain a dragon … of course I couldn't actually slay a dragon, most of them are my cousins… but if we make it look like I've slain one then maybe the King will be so impressed with my bravery that he'll get over me being a dragon and…'

'DAVE!' Albrecht cut him off. 'That sounds a lot like cheating to me! You are not acting like the Dave I know, you're acting like a dummkopf knight like Gnasty!'

'That's the whole point!' shouted Dave, starting to get angry. 'I don't want to be Dave! I want to be a KNIGHT! But how am I going to do that now eh? How am I going to do anything?! I'm no good at being a dragon and now I can't be a knight.'

'Now Dave, when I became separated from the Foreign Legion and was lost in the Mutabu Desert and was forced to eat a cactus…there was one important thing I learnt…'

Never have I experienced anything so pointy.

'ENOUGH OF YOUR STUPID STORIES!'
yelled Dave. 'Everyone knows they are lies! A goat
could never do all those things. You're delusional!'

Albrecht looked hurt but Dave wasn't done.

'You mad old goat, making me do all your crazy
plans and bossing me around all the time. And
you know what? You're not even that glossy!'

That was the final straw for Albrecht. 'I
condition my coat daily as you well know David!
Fine. I can see you don't think you need a trusty
steed any more so you can do it all alone.'

'And you do smell goaty,' added Dave.

'IT'S A CHARMING MUSK! The saddest
thing is Dave, you're a better knight when you're
acting like Dave, not following the stupid knight
book and trying to be like those Dummköpfe back
in the castle! Also, I HATE your special hat!'

'How dare you!' said Dave.

'You're a DUMMKOPF!' shouted Albrecht.

'No, you're a DUMMKOPF!' Dave bawled back.

And they both stormed off in different
directions.

Meanwhile back in the castle the King was wandering the corridors with Albrecht's shoe.

'Madam? Madam! I have your shoe! Where are you? Would you like to go for dinner? Let us never be parted! OOOPH!' he said as he bumped straight into Sir Gnasty.

'Ah! Gnasty,' said the King. 'Have you seen the most exquisite lady around here? She has but one single shoe, the hoofiest of feet and smells kind of goaty.'

'Hmmm, I think I might have seen her hiding in this huge sack here,' said Gnasty whipping a sack out from behind his back.

'Excellent. Top job my good man. At last! My love we shall be together!' The King toddled into the sack.

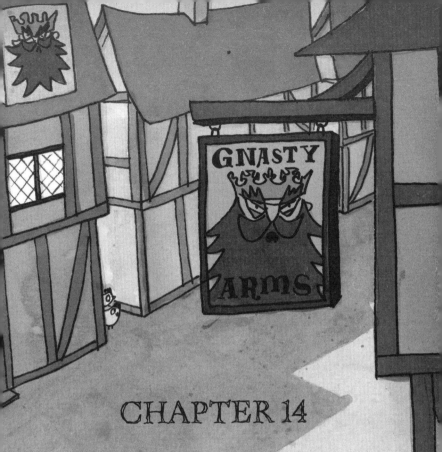

CHAPTER 14

Two weeks later …

After taking the King prisoner, Gnasty crowned himself Supreme Evil Overlord and ruled with an iron fist. Everything from brawling to rat-on-a-stick was banned and all jammy dodgers confiscated. In Castletown the peasants have become restless and unhappy. This can't go on.

Inside the Dragon's Head (recently renamed the Gnasty Arms) the atmosphere was glum.

'Rubella, you're a barmaid, do you know if there's rat in this pint?' asked the Bearded Lady.

'Who knows?' said Rubella. 'Everything's got worse since Gnasty came to power. The drinks, the food. I'm not even sure there's any real rat in the rat-on-a-stick any more so you'd be lucky if there's some in your drink.'

Rubbish.

♪ Gnasty ♪
We all hate
Gnasty ♫

Rubella, how's being a barmaid since Gnasty banished you from the castle?
GNASTY IS WATCHING YOU!
GNASTY BANS BOILS
AND CARBUNCLES

'And whacking injuries are up 200% since Gnasty put in place his "Everything Will Be Punished With A Whack" policy,' added the Bearded Lady. 'On the up side my business is doing so well I can finally afford a candy cane conservatory.'

'And Albrecht! All he's done since Dave left is sit in the corner and drink mouthwash.'

'And what about your father the King? I hear he's been imprisoned in the dungeons.'

'Oh he'll be fine,' said Rubella. 'He loves slop, especially the XXX Super Hot.'

'This isn't right. Something's got to be done.'

'Let's form a resistance,' whispered Rubella, immediately looking around for spies.

'The peasants' resistance!'

'The peasant and *princess* resistance.'

'Yeah sure. But what we really need is someone who can save the King and take down Gnasty.'

Rubella looked concerned. 'But all the other knights have gone into hiding because they're far too afraid of him and even if they weren't he's stronger than everyone.'

'Then we need someone who doesn't need brute

strength. What happened to Dave? He got things done without whacking.'

'But Dave is a dragon!'

'Who cares if he's a dragon,' said the Bearded Lady. 'Everyone thought I couldn't be a doctor just because I'm a bearded lady, so I don't see why Dave can't be a knight just because he's a Dragon. Plus he was a nice guy.'

'Good point,' said Rubella. 'How will we get him back though? I heard he joined a troupe of travelling actors.'

'There's only one person who can convince Dave to come back,' said the Bearded Lady, turning to look at the corner of the room.

Fräulein! Fräulein! more minty fresh bitte!

MOUTH WASH

143

Rubella raised an eyebrow, but they called Albrecht over anyway. He stumbled over reeking of peppermint and wasn't impressed by their plan.

'Pleh! I don't associate with the likes of Dave any more. No more dummköpfe for Albrecht! I adventure solo now.'

The Bearded Lady was having none of it. 'Albrecht, even if you're not going to be friends we need him for the sake of the kingdom. Just get him back.'

In a field not too far from Castletown, Dave was getting fired.

I really thought I couldn't go wrong casting a dragon as a dragon! But Dave you're really EXCEPTIONALLY BAD. This is the last time you get booed off stage. YOU'RE FIRED!

Dave sighed, took off his costume head and went to sit on a rock away from the other players.

'HULLO!'

'WAAAHHHH!' said Dave falling off his rock. 'Albrecht! What do you think you're doing here?'

'I've come to take you back Dave! Gnasty is destroying the kingdom and we need your knight skills to defeat him. But that doesn't mean we're friends! You were very mean about my glossiness.'

'Oh here we go again, always telling me what to do! Anyway I can't. I don't have what it takes to be a knight, like I didn't have what it takes to be a dragon. Now I'm not even any good at pretending to be a dragon. And I'm definitely not coming back so I can be bossed around by you again.'

'The Dave I knew would at least try. I'll get you back to that town or I'll eat my hintern!'

So even though Albrecht couldn't convince Dave, they headed back to Castletown anyway.

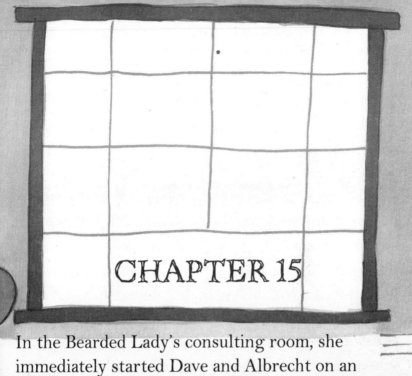

CHAPTER 15

In the Bearded Lady's consulting room, she immediately started Dave and Albrecht on an intensive session of couples counselling so they could talk about their feelings.

'Dave said some very mean things to me,' said Albrecht folding his arms and looking pouty. 'About my coat, my smell, and all my stories!'

'OK good progress,' said the Bearded Lady, scribbling notes on her pad. 'And Dave, what made you unhappy?'

'Albrecht's so bossy! He's always saying we must do this thing because that's how he did it when he was locked in the jungle or we have to use his GENIUS because it worked when he was in hiding in the frozen North, bah bah bah.'

'We're doing some very good work here,' said the Bearded Lady. 'Dave, I think it might help if you understood each other a little better. Why don't you tell Albrecht about your childhood?'

So Dave explained about the dragon caves, never being a very good dragon and the summer he spent with Great Aunt Maud the librarian.

'And she gave me a book to take home!' said Dave. 'It was called "Fuzzy Bunny's Big Adventure". You know I was never a very dragony dragon but somehow when I had this book it was all okay.'

'I took it everywhere with me.'

'But one day something terrible happened.'

'Mein Dave?!' said Albrecht 'You can breathe FIRE?!'

'Yes, but I don't like to talk about it. It was the worst day of my life!' said Dave. 'I suppose since then I've been looking for another book that'll make everything OK. Also, I really hate butterflies.'

'Great!' said the Bearded Lady. 'Now Dave, what do you know about Albrecht's past?'

'Loads. He never stops talking about himself.'

'But how did a goat come to have all those adventures, Dave? Albrecht, would you like to explain?'

As a child Albrecht was just a normal goat, though perhaps more adventurous than most.

Until one day he was bought by a wizard : . .

. . . who had plans for him.

The outcome was unusual.

When he had the chance,
Albrecht escaped.

But once he got home, things just weren't the same.

So Albrecht set out to see the world, and perhaps even find a place where he'd fit in.

Albrecht had adventures. A LOT of adventures. And he got a taste for it.

Fisticuffs!

Eventually Albrecht started to feel his age and realized that he'd never really had a chance just to be a goat. So Albrecht retired to a local goat farm to spend some time getting back to his roots.

The problem was he'd forgotten how boring his roots were.

And that's when Dave came along.

'So you see, Dave, it was you who reignited Albrecht's sense of adventure with the chance to help you. Maybe he comes across as bossy because he doesn't want you to make mistakes?'

'You had to leave your family too?' said Dave.

'I don't like to talk about it,' said Albrecht.

Dave was shocked by the idea that there was anything Albrecht didn't want to talk about but he'd started to feel a bit guilty. 'I'm sorry Albrecht. I guess I was pretty mean when you were just trying to help.'

'Don't worry mein Dave,' said Albrecht. 'When I was trapped on a desert island with only a hamster for company...'

'NO, NO! No stories! Too soon!' Dave stuck his fingers in his ears.

'OK, OK,' said Albrecht. 'I'm sorry about my bossiness. It's just because you could be an über knight if you...'

'But I can't be a knight. I'm a dragon and if you read the book...'

'You think too much about what the rules are. You saved a Princess, ja? Stopped peasants rioting? Won a tournament? But you didn't do it the knight way with whacking and kissing and moustaches. You did it the Dave way, with GENIUS!'

'So,' added the Bearded Lady, 'is there any reason why you're not a knight?'

'Well, um…' Actually, Dave couldn't think of a reason. So what if he didn't slay a dragon? Slaying things isn't good or kind or wise like a knight should be. Maybe he *was* good at this.

'You…might have a point,' said Dave quietly.

'JA!' said Albrecht. 'You can save the kingdom and do it the Dave way.'

'Well I suppose if there are innocent people in danger I should be brave and try.'

'Excellent! I think this has been a very productive session,' said the Bearded Lady. 'Now GROUP HUG and my bill will be in the post.'

You can stop hugging now.

'Right my trusty steed,' said Dave. 'Let's go and save the King, and show Gnasty who's really a knight!'

'Ja!' said Albrecht. 'But first, Dave, I think you're missing something.'

Finally, I've got me some new armour.

Hey Ironpants! Fancy a rematch?

KAW!

e wants more
mmy
odgers!

let's grow
stinging
nettles!

The
brambles
are doing
really well.

CHAPTER 16

Once Dave and Albrecht reached the castle
walls they started to think getting in might be
a little tricky.

KEEP
OUT!

'How are we going to get in there?' said Dave. 'We'd need a whole ARMY!'

'Worry not,' said Albrecht. 'I have an idea.'

'I have sent for help. Now we must wait,' said Albrecht.

'O-kaaay. What kind of help?' asked Dave.

'Just some people I know from my travels.'

Dave still wasn't sure how true all Albrecht's stories really were, but he didn't want to upset him again. 'So, why are seagulls carrying messages for you?'

'I'm their King,' said Albrecht. 'It's a funny story really…'

'DON'T EVEN START!' said Dave.

Meanwhile, inside the castle things weren't going to plan in the throne room.

'PEACOCKS?!' yelled Gnasty. 'I wanted sharks! All evil hideouts must have sharks! Why did you get these prissy birds?!'

'Um,' said Alf. 'These were the nearest thing the pet shop had to sharks. Perhaps we could dress them up with fins and…'

'Oooh!' said the King from his little cage suspended from the ceiling. 'You must give me the name of that pet shop. I'd like a few more to go in the garden too…'

'SHUT UP! This isn't your castle any more tiny man! Alan, get him some slop. That always keeps him quiet. Linda, add peacocks to the list of banned things,' said Gnasty.

'Oooh yes! XXX Super Hot Chilli slop for me!' said the King.

Gnasty gave up on the peacocks and lowered himself into the throne. 'Now, Army of Evil! I need you to be on your guard. Things have been too easy for us so far. It's just too quiet. I want everyone on patrol and our defences tightened. I've got a feeling something's going on…'

The sun had risen high into the sky as Dave sat waiting under the bush. To be honest he was starting to give up hope.

'There's no one coming is there?' he said.

Albrecht peered at his watch. 'They should be here soon. I gave the gulls very specific instructions but sometimes they can get confused or distracted by chips.'

Then Dave noticed a rumbling coming from the bottom of the ridge. He scrambled out of the bush and peered into the distance. What was that? He thought he saw something . . . wait . . . is that a whale?!

It was a whale. A whale being pushed along in a cart by a troupe of straining mud wrestlers. A worrying number of ballet dancers pranced past them followed by the foreign legion, a tribe of cannibalistic sheep-men and an old man who could only have been the Snakes and Ladders Master. All people from Albrecht's stories!

On top of that, Dave spied a few familiar faces. Ahead of a group of already-rioting peasants the Bearded Lady was striding along with a first aid kit and a club. The other knights had come out of hiding having obviously been forced there by Rubella who was prodding them in the right direction with a stick. Even the witch had come along, occasionally blowing kisses at Sir Ironpants as she went. It was a real, if kind of weird, ARMY!

Dave ran up to Albrecht. 'I can't believe it! Your stories were all true! You have had a lot of adventures.' Dave thought about this and wrinkled his nose. 'Really strange adventures. I mean the ballet? Really? Did you really have a fling with the lady whale? And… oh gosh that thing about your tail…' Dave decided not to think about it too hard.

'Ja, I did say,' said Albrecht. 'But we must not get distracted, Dave. This is not the first rebellion I've led so I shall make a rousing speech to the army and then we'll attack the castle.'

'Right, so then I'll sneak in, free the King and get Gnasty while he's distracted.'

'Über plan! Now Dave, I've got something for you.'

Albrecht rummaged in his pockets and pulled out the book. 'I saved it the night of the feast. I thought you might want it now.'

Where exactly are your pockets?

Dave looked at the book. 'Well, thank you. But… do I need it?'

'I know you'll do the right thing with it. Now there's no time to lose.'

Albrecht ran down the hill to greet some old friends, and address his massive, weird army.

He leapt on top of the lady whale and began to shout. 'Guten tag! I am Albrecht the trustiest of all the steeds! Today we overthrow the Evil Overlord Gnasty! He may whack us, he may take our boils, he may ruin our rat-on-a-stick but he'll never take our FREEDOM!'

CHARGE!

As the army charged the castle gates, Dave took
the opportunity to disappear back into the drains.
He was getting to know them rather well by now.
After a few wrong turns Dave popped up through
the ladies.

'Oh. Ah. Hello Linda.'

After locking Linda in the loo (he felt a bit
bad about that but he knew she was a bit of a
snitch), Dave snuck through the castle corridors
hiding from peacocks and panicking Army of Evil

members who were shouting things like, 'We're
being attacked by a whale! A WHALE!'

As Dave got closer to the throne room he

started to feel his legs go weak and the familiar feeling of needing a wee. How was he going to beat a massive knight like Gnasty? If only he'd had a chance to read the single combat bit of the book in more detail… no wait, that's what the old Dave would do. Sir Dave would just go in there, be brave, trust his instincts, and try not to wee himself.

He pushed open the throne room door and peeked inside. Dave let out a sigh of relief when he realized it was empty apart from the King in his cage.

'Ahoy there, David!' said the King. 'You're a sight for sore eyes. How's Rubella? Would you like some of this slop? It's the XXX Super Hot.'

Dave had an idea. 'Stop eating that slop, Sir! You need to throw the bowl at the bars.'

'But it's delicious! One should not waste good slop.'

'We can get you more slop later Your Highness! Do you want to escape or not?'

'Oh yes escape! How thrilling.' The King flung the slop at the bars. With a sizzle and a SLOP the bars melted away.

The King hopped down and Dave looked curious. 'How were you eating that?!'

'It reminds me of the food we used to have at boarding school,' said the King wistfully. 'Although we only used to get Classic Brown slop.'

That sounds even worse than dragon training, thought Dave. 'Hang on a second, Sire, we still have Gnasty to think about.'

'*MwahahaHA!* Dave. Oh I'm so pleased you came back.'

Dave spun around.

'Look at you cowering there with your stupid book,' said Gnasty with a worrying grin on his face. 'Still trying to be a knight are you? Well there'll be no more of your ridiculous dreams because I'm going to squish you so hard the jailer will make slop with what's left.'

Gnasty hauled up his mace for the final whack. Dave was more afraid than ever. He did not want to become Premium Dave Slop. Sure that this time he really was going to have an accident Dave did something without even really thinking. He narrowed his eyes, pulled back his arm, and flung the book at Gnasty.

Gnasty's eyes crossed, and he fell to the floor with a huge **THWUMP!**

CHAPTER 17

HUZZAH! Castletown was celebrating! The King had declared a whole day of feasting in honour of Gnasty's defeat and Dave finally getting his knighthood. The market square was bustling with peasants guzzling rat-on-a-stick, listening to Dr Hilarity's terrible one-man joke show, occasionally having a little brawl, and being patched up by the Bearded Lady.

Gnasty was pottering about the square with his peacocks. He'd been a changed man since his knock on the head and was a lot easier to be around. He'd also become very fond of the peacocks. Everyone thought he seemed fairly happy, if a bit muddled.

Pretty birds.

A stage had been built in front of the castle. As the bell tolled noon, the King climbed onto the podium followed by Rubella. He scrambled up onto his box and began his speech.

'Ladies, gentlemen, knights, and peasants! This day of celebration is to honour Sir Dave and his

bravery in saving both myself and the kingdom.
Today I shall officially knight him! First though I
have something important to say. As long as they
don't eat anyone's home, set anything on fire and
keep the knitting to a minimum, from this day
onwards Castletown will be a dragon-friendly
town!'

The crowd gave a big cheer and Dave shot
Albrecht a big grin.

'And one last thing. Does anyone know who this
shoe belongs to?' The King held up the shoe that
Albrecht had dropped when running from the
feast.

Sniff!
So
goaty!

All that time
I was in that
cage she
was all I
thought
of.

'Ah there it is!' said Albrecht bouncing up onto the stage and taking the shoe. 'I wanted to wear this pair for the ceremony.' He put the shoe on.

'You!' said the King 'You're my ladylove? But, you're a goat! Well, I swore that I would marry whomever that shoe does fit and after all you're still the woman, or goat, I fell in love

with. And I admit there is a strange allure about you. Do you still have that pineapple? We can make it work, can't we?'

'You are so embarrassing,' said Rubella holding her head in her hands.

'Ermm,' said Albrecht. 'I do not think this is going to work. I'm, er, in a relationship.'

Dave raised an eyebrow. That was news to him.

'That's disappointing.' The King looked genuinely upset. 'Oh well, good luck to you. Anyway, to show my gratitude I have devised the perfect reward. Dave, I would like to offer you Rubella's hand in marriage!'

Dave's mouth dropped open. This could be awkward.

Rubella stepped forward and held up a hand for silence. 'No, Father, I love another. I intend to marry my darling Gilbert!' Rubella held up a frog who said, 'She loves me for who I am!'

'Oh, right. What? We'll talk about this later young lady!' The King was starting to look quite flustered. 'Er, sorry about this Dave. I think just the knighthood will have to do for now.'

Dave couldn't have been more relieved.

'Step forward Dave!'

So Dave ascended the stage.

After the ceremony, once the party was in full swing, the other knights were all busy congratulating Sir Dave.

'Good work old boy!' said Sir Mightybrow, accidentally clapping Sir Ironpants on the back because he'd misplaced his glasses again.

'Now that you're a proper knight like the rest of us you should really think about getting a proper steed. I know a used steed dealer who can get you a really glossy one,' said Sir Snoz, giving Albrecht a disdainful look.

'Yes!' agreed Sir Butterball spraying pie crumbs all over Dave. 'Whoever heard of a knight riding a goat! Hawhaw!'

Dave paused for a moment and then turned to look Albrecht in the eye. 'Well I don't remember there ever being a knight who was a dragon, so I see no reason why there shouldn't be a steed who's a goat.'

That shut the other knights up.

Dave gave them a little grin and hopped onto Albrecht's back. Albrecht turned and waggled his wooden tail rudely before galloping off into the sunset where they would have their own party. A better party, with a whale, and bareknuckle board games, and Albrecht's ex troupe of ballet dancers pulling out all their moves, and absolutely *no* slop whatsoever.

CHAPTER 18

To make up for Rubella being engaged to a frog, the King gave Dave and Albrecht a fancy house on the edge of Castletown.

Albrecht plonked another box of Dave's books, that his parents had sent from the Dragons' Cave, down onto the kitchen table and looked around contentedly.

'You know I think house sharing will be wunderbar!' said Albrecht. 'Do you like washing up meine Dave?'

Dave was busy looking through Knighthood for Beginners so wasn't really listening. Albrecht went over and put an arm around Dave and gave him a squeeze.

'And you did it! You really became a knight. I could not be more proud of you!' He was looking dangerously teary.

'Yes I am pleased,' said Dave looking distracted.

'What is it Dave? Are you not happy?' Albrecht asked.

'I am happy,' said Dave 'but now that it's all over I think I enjoyed the adventure more than getting the actual knighthood.'

'Ahah!' said Albrecht. 'You see this is how it starts, the taste for adventure! You know there can always be more?'

'There can?'

'Ja! We could ride off into the sunset now and find another adventure! But you can't ride on my back any more. The aching is most terrible.'

'Have you been using that cream the Bearded Lady gave you? Did you know her real name is Mildred?'

'Yes of course I have been using the cream. I was supposed to eat it ja?'

'You might want to read the label,' said Dave. 'Funny you should say that about adventure though. I found this page at the very end of the book…'

Albrecht considered the page. 'Well, we'd best find a bookshop!'

YOU might also enjoy...

MY LIFE IN BOILS BY BOIL MAN

FROM THE CREATOR OF RAT-ON-A-STICK

RAT RECIPES

MASTER snakes AND LADDERS

BY GAMESMASTER

Accounting for Beginners

WIZARDING for Beginners

learn basic magic and beard styling in this step-by-step guide.

CASTLE MANAGEMENT

In all good book shops NOW!

AND THEY ALL LIVED HAPPILY EVER AFTER.

Gnasty became a full-time peacock farmer and never tried to whack anyone ever again.

Rubella went against her father's wishes and married Gilbert the frog. The family were very disappointed when he didn't turn into a prince, but they put in a new pond and had to admit the couple seemed very happy.

Gnasty's Army of Evil disbanded and formed a barbershop quartet. They're now touring the kingdom, but rumour says Linda may go solo due to artistic differences.

LA LA LA LA LA LAA!

The witch and Sir Ironpants broke up but found a shared interest in the construction industry and started the Gingerbread Building Co. together specializing in candy cane conservatories.

The King never won the heart of his ladylove and to this day still writes terrible poetry about her.

Rat-on-a-stick guy branched out into snake-on-a-stick. It's proving popular despite the occasional poisoning.

Boil Man's boil burst
in a freak cart accident.
It was a bad day for
everyone.

Dame Hilda left the
castle and is now
pursuing a successful
opera career.

Mildred the Bearded
Lady is Castletown's
most popular doctor
ever. She's started
a support group for
young girls with
moustaches.

Dave's parents were
very pleased to hear
about his success as a
knight even though it
violates Dragon Lore.

They came to visit Dave and Albrecht who were both given a lot of new scarfs, mittens, and a lovely hat during their stay.

After meeting again at the battle, the Lady Whale and Albrecht decided to give it another go. Albrecht keeps trying to have her round for dinner, which is challenging because she's much, much bigger than the front door.

Dave and Albrecht have continued to house share, although Dave seems to end up doing all the washing up and Albrecht keeps putting his hooves on the furniture. They're sure there'll be more adventures coming their way soon.

10%OFF

Armour Coupon

REDEEMABLE AT ANY GOOD ARMOURERS
NOT TO BE USED WITH ANY OTHER OFFERS

FREE STEED SERVICE

FAST

GLOSSY

Albrecht's German
for Dummköpfe

Aufwachen – wake up

Dummkopf – fool, blockhead (singular)

Dummköpfe – fools, blockheads (plural)

Fräulein – Miss, young lady

Guten tag – Good day

Ich kann sprechen – I can speak

Ja – Yes (pronounced Yah)

Kleine – little

Kleiner Drache – little dragon

Kleine Suppe Werfer – small soup thrower

Können sie mich verstehen? – Can you understand me?

Mein – my

Mein Dorf Esser – my village eater

Meine Hintern – my bottom

Meine Gott! Ich kann sprechen! – My God! I can talk!

Mein Dave – my Dave

Mein kleiner grüner (friend) – my little green (friend)

Sauerkraut – pickled cabbage

Schnell – quickly

Über –outstanding, utmost, extremely

Wunderbar - wonderful

Elys is an author and illustrator currently living and working in Cambridge. She works predominantly with ink, newfangled digital witchcraft, and coloured pencils, of which she is the proud owner of 178 but can never seem to find a sharpener. When not doing pictures and making things up, Elys enjoys growing cacti, collecting pocket watches, and eating excessive amounts of fondant fancies.

Knighthood for Beginners is Elys Dolan's first young fiction book, her hilarious picture books have been shortlisted for *The Roald Dahl Funny Prize, Waterstones Children's Book Prize,* and nominated for the *Kate Greenaway Medal.*

More from Elys Dolan

STEVEN SEAGULL
ACTION HERO

Mr Bunny's Chocolate Factory

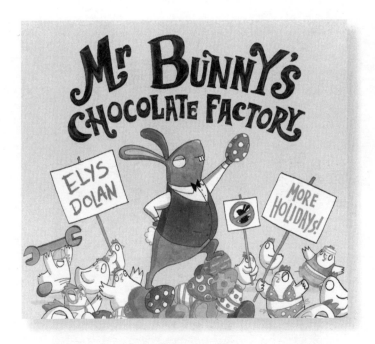

The CLOCKWORK DRAGON

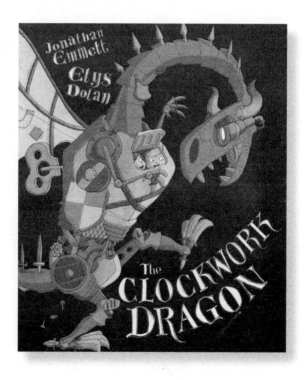